David Forrester

WOD's 2.0

A Collection of More Than 200 Great WOD's

Disclaimer

This book is solely for educational purposes and should be taken as such. The author takes no responsibility for any misappropriation of the contents stated in this book and thus cannot and will not be held liable for any damages incurred because of it. Like any sport involving speed, equipment, balance and environmental factors, this sport poses some inherent risk. The authors and publisher advise readers to take full responsibility for their safety and know their limits. Before practicing the skills described in this book, be sure that your equipment is well maintained, and do not take risks beyond your level of experience, aptitude, training, and comfort level.

WOD's 2.0

About This Book

More than 200 WOD's in one book! This book was made to let you easily access a complete list of WOD's from a single source - *WOD's 2.0*. You can take these workouts with you to any place–the gym, a park, your local "cross-training box" or simply use it at the convenience of your home.

In this book you'll find all types of WOD's – WOD's for beginners, the benchmark girls WOD's, hero WOD's and WOD's-To-Go (WOD's that don't require equipment). If you're a beginner looking to try these workouts or you are already an experienced veteran looking for new challenges, you will find what you're looking for in this book. Plus, you will find some motivational quotes at the end of the book!

So what are you waiting for? Go through the book, choose a WOD and get your heart pumping!

WOD's 2.0

Table of Contents

Introduction – What are WOD's?

A'W.O.D.' is an acronym for 'Workout Of the Day'. In some fitness communities, each day there is a workout that is posted online or assigned to the trainees. Quite often they are rather brutal. They test the limits of your strength, endurance and speed. But if you are a beginner don't worry, there are plenty of easier WOD's to get you started in this special fitness regime. Often these workouts are completed in a group setting where you can test yourself against others.

As you go through the various types of WOD's in this book, you will get to know what makes these workouts different from regular workouts in the gym.

WOD's 2.0

How to Use This Book

The WOD's have been divided into 4 categories:

> ➤ Benchmark WOD's
> ➤ Beginner WOD's
> ➤ Hero WOD's
> ➤ WODs-to-go (no equipment needed)

In terms of difficulty, the beginner WOD's and WOD's-To-Go are the easiest. The benchmark girls WOD's range from medium to hard difficulty and the hero WOD's are very hard workouts.

Understanding the WOD's

Example

Fran

Thruster 95 lbs

Pull-ups

Goal: Complete for time.

Instructions: Complete 21-15-9 reps of the exercises.

Explanation

This WOD is called "Fran". It consists of two exercises: a thruster with 95 lbs weight and pull-ups.

You must complete 21 thrusters, 21 pull-ups, 15 thrusters, 15 pull-ups and 9 thrusters, 9 pull-ups.

The goal of this workout is to complete the exercises as quickly as possible. That means that you should record your results and record them every time you attempt this WOD. This way you can compare your results and see your progress.

IMPORTANT Tip: Do not forget to warm up before doing the workouts!

Warning: These WOD's haven't been created by me. The workouts in this book are meant to be used as guidelines. Please consult with a certified trainer on how to perform the exercises used in this book to avoid injury.

The Benchmark Girls WOD's

Introduction

The *benchmark girls* WOD's are foundational WOD's made to test your fitness development over time by comparing new results with past results. For instance, if you improve your Fran (which is, by the way, the most infamous among the benchmark WOD's) time, you will have improved your overall fitness level.

When completeing WOD's, results are measured by breaking old personal records and setting new ones on lifts, skills, and WOD's such as the Fran. This is the fundamental methodology with the WOD's - measuring results and improving them over time. In the following pages you will find a list of WOD's known as "The Girls."

The List of WODs

- Angie (15)
- Annie (15)
- Barbara (15)
- Chelsea (16)
- Cindy (16)
- Diane (16)
- Elizabeth (16)
- Eva (17)
- Fran (17)
- Grace (17)
- Helen (18)
- Isabel (18)
- Jackie (18)
- Karen (18)
- Kelly (19)
- Linda (19)
- Lynne (19)
- Mary (20)
- Nancy (20)
- Nicole (20)

More WOD's That Can Be Used As Benchmark Workouts

- Filthy Fifty (21)
- Nasty Girls (21)
- Tabata This (22)
- Tabata Something Else (22)
- Quarter Gone Bad (22)

Angie

100 Pull-ups

100 Push-ups

100 Sit-ups

100 Squats

Goal: Complete in the shortest amount of time possible.

Instructions: Complete all repetitions of each exercise before moving on to the next.

Annie

Double-unders

Sit-ups

Goal: Complete for time.

Instructions: 50-40-30-20 and 10 rep rounds.

Barbara

20 Pull-ups

30 Push-ups

40 Sit-ups

50 Squats

Goal: Complete for time.

Instructions: Complete a total of 5 rounds and time each of them. Rest exactly 3 minutes between each round.

Chelsea

5 Pull-ups

10 Push-ups

15 Squats

Goal: Complete for rounds.

Instructions: Each minute on the minute for 30 min.

Cindy

5 Pull-ups

10 Push-ups

15 Squats

Goal: Complete as many rounds as possible in 20 min.

Instructions: Complete as many rounds of the exercises listed as possible, within 20 minutes.

Diane

Deadlift 225 lbs

Handstand push-ups

Goal: Complete for time.

Instructions: 21-15-9 reps

Elizabeth

Clean 135 lbs

Ring Dips

Goal: Complete for time.

Instructions: Complete 21-15-9 reps of both exercises as quickly as possible.

Eva

Run 800 meters

2 pood KB swing, 30 reps

30 pullups

Goal: Complete for time.

Instructions: Complete 5 rounds of these three exercises.

Fran

Thruster 95 lbs

Pull-ups

Goal: Complete for time.

Instructions: Complete 21-15-9 reps of the exercises.

Grace

Clean and Jerk 135 lbs

Goal: Complete for time.

Instructions: Complete 30 reps of the exercise for time.

Helen

400 meter run

1.5 pood Kettlebell swing x 21

Pull-ups 12 reps

Goal: Complete for time.

Instructions: Complete 3 roundsfor time.

Isabel

Snatch 135 pounds

Goal: Complete for time.

Instructions: Do 30 reps of the exercise for time.

Jackie

1000 meter row

Thruster 45 lbs (50 reps)

Pull-ups (30 reps)

Goal: Complete for time.

Instructions: Complete all repetitions of each exercise before moving to the next.

Karen

Wall-ball 150 shots

Goal: Complete for time.

Instructions: Do 150 Wall-Ball shots for time.

Kelly

Run 400 meters

30 box jump, 24 inch box

30 Wall ball shots, 20 pound ball

Goal: Complete for time.

Instructions: Complete 5 rounds for time.

Linda

Dead lift 1 1/2 BW

Bench BW

Clean 3/4 BW

Goal: Complete for time.

Instructions: 10/9/8/7/6/5/4/3/2/1 rep rounds for time.

Lynne

Bodyweight bench press (as much weight on the bar as you weigh)

Pull-ups

Goal: 5 rounds for max reps.

Instructions: Complete 5 rounds and do as many reps as possible. Three is No time component to this WOD.

Mary

5 Handstand push-ups

10 1-legged squats

15 Pull-ups

Goal: Complete as many rounds as possible within time frame.

Instructions: Complete as many rounds of the exercises as possible within 20 min.

Nancy

400 meter run

Overhead squat 95 lbs x 15

Goal: Complete for time.

Instructions: Complete 5 rounds for time.

Nicole

Run 400 meters

Max rep Pull-ups

Goal: Complete as many rounds as possible in 20 minutes.

Instructions: Complete as many rounds as possible in 20 minutes and record number of pull-ups completed for each round.

More WOD's That Can Be Used As Benchmark Workouts

Filthy Fifty

50 Box jumps (24")

50 Jumping pull-ups

50 Kettlebell swings (1 pd)

50 Walking lunges

50 Knees to elbows

50 Push press (45 lb)

50 Back extensions

50 Wall ball shots (20 lb)

50 Burpees

50 Double-unders

Goal: Complete for time.

Instructions: Do all the excercises as quickly as you can.

Nasty Girls

50 Squats

7 Muscle-ups

10 Hang power-cleans (135 lb)

Goal: Complete 3 rounds for time.

Instructions: Do 3 rounds of all the exercises as quickly as you can.

Tabata This

Tabata Squats

Tabata Rows

Tabata Pull-ups

Tabata Sit-ups

Tabata Push-ups

Goal: Complete for reps.

Instructions: Do 20 seconds of work/10 seconds rest x 8 rounds. Do each exercise wth no rest between exercises. Your total reps from all exercises (32 intervals in total) are the score.

Tabata Something Else

Tabata Pull-ups

Tabata Push-ups

Tabata Sit-ups

Tabata Squats

Goal: Complete for reps.

Instructions: Do 20 seconds of work/10 seconds rest x8 rounds. Do each exercise wth no rest between exercises. Your total reps from all exercises (32 intervals in total) are the score.

Quarter Gone Bad

135 lb Thruster (15 seconds)

Rest (45 seconds)

50 lb Weighted Pull-up (15 seconds)

Rest (45 seconds)

Burpees (15 seconds)

Rest (45 seconds)

Goal: Complete for reps.

Instruction: Do 5 rounds for total reps.

Beginner WOD's

Introduction

WOD's for beginners are simple and easy workouts made for people who are getting started with WOD's or people getting back into "the game". These WOD's will help you to get started and ease into the more rigorous WOD's which will follow later on. Also, most of them don't even require any equipment.

As many of these WOD's have no "official names", they have been named after the main exercises that they include. This way it will be easier for you to repeatedly access them when you need to.

The List of WODs

- ➢ Modified Fran (27)
- ➢ Modified Chelsea (27)
- ➢ Modified Mary (27)
- ➢ Modified Lynne (28)
- ➢ Modified Angie (28)
- ➢ Modified Barbara (28)
- ➢ Modified Karen (29)
- ➢ Skipping, Squats, Box step-ups (29)
- ➢ Burpees, squats, push-ups, squats, burpees (29)
- ➢ Box step-ups, Kettleswings, squats (30)
- ➢ Row, push preses (30)
- ➢ Burpees, squats, situps (30)
- ➢ Jumping jacks, airs quats, push-ups (30)
- ➢ Lunges, push-ups (31)
- ➢ Jumping jacks, sit-ups (31)
- ➢ Pushups, sit ups, air squats (31)
- ➢ Lunges, push-ups (32)
- ➢ Run 200m, Pull-ups (32)
- ➢ Run 200m, squats (32)
- ➢ Pushups for time (32)

Modified Fran

21 Burpees

21 Squats

15 Burpees

15 Squats

9 Burpees

9 Squats

Goal: Complete for time.

Instructions: Complete **1 round** of the exercises as quickly as possible.

Modified Chelsea

4 Chin ups

8 Push ups

12 Squats

Goal: Complete for rounds.

Instructions: Complete exercises 10 minutes, on every minute.

Modified Mary

3 Handstand push-ups

8 1-legged squats

10 Pull-ups

Goal: Complete as many rounds as possible within time frame.

Instructions: Complete as many rounds of the exercises as possible within 10 minutes.

Modified Lynne

Half of bodyweight bench press (half your bodyweight the on bar)

Max Pull-ups

Goal: 3 rounds for max reps.

Instructions: Complete **3 rounds** and do as many reps as possible. Three is no time component to this WOD.

Modified Angie

50 Pull-ups

50 Push-ups

50 Sit-ups

50 Squats

Goal: Complete in the shortest amount of time possible.

Instructions: Complete all repetitions of each exercise before moving to the next. Complete as quickly as possible.

Modified Barbara

15 Pull-ups

25 Push-ups

30 Sit-ups

35 Squats

Goal: Complete **3 rounds** for time

Instructions: Complete a total of 3 rounds and time each of them. Rest exactly 3 minutes between each round.

Modified Karen

Wall-ball 100 shots

Goal: Complete for time.

Instructions: Complete **100 Wall-Ball shots** as quickly as possible.

Skipping, Squats, Box Step ups

45 Seconds Skipping

45 Seconds of Squats

45 Seconds of Box Step Ups

Goal: Complete for time.

Instructions: Complete **5 rounds** as quickly as possible.

Burpees, squats, push-ups, squats, burpees

10 Burpees

20 Squats

30 Push Ups

20 Squats

10 Burpees

Goal: Complete for time.

Instructions: Complete **a single round** as quickly as possible.

Box step ups, Kettle swings, squats

10 Box step ups

10 Kettle Swings

10 Squats

Goal: Complete for time.

Instructions: Complete **4 rounds** as quickly as possible.

Row, push preses

Row 750 meters

10 Push Presses

Goal: Complete for time.

Instructions: Complete **3 rounds** as quickly as possible.

Burpees, squats, situps

10 burpees

20 squats

30 situps

Goal: Complete for time.

Instructions: Complete **3 rounds** as quickly as possible.

Jumping jacks, air squats, push-ups

50 jumping jacks

20 air squats

15 push-ups

Goal: Complete for time.

Instructions: Complete **2 rounds** for time.

Lunges, push-ups

20 lunges

10 push-ups

Goal: Complete for time.

Instructions: Complete **5 rounds** as quickly as possible.

Jumping jacks, sit-ups

20 jumping jacks

10 push-ups

Goal: Complete for time.

Instructions: Complete **5 rounds** as quickly as possible.

Push ups, sit ups, air squats

15 push ups

15 sit-ups

15 air squats

Goal: Complete for time.

Instructions: Complete **5 rounds** as quickly as possible.

Lunges, push-ups

20 Lunges

15 push-ups

Goal: Complete for time.

Instructions: Complete **5 rounds** as quickly as possible.

Run 200m, Pull ups

Run 200 meters

5 pull ups

Goal: Complete for time.

Instructions: Complete **3 rounds** as quickly as possible.

Run 200m, squats

Run 200 meters

15 squats

Goal: Complete for time.

Instructions: Complete **3 rounds** as quickly as possible.

Push ups for time.

100 push ups

Goal: Complete for time.

Instructions: Complete the exercise as quickly as possible.

WOD's 2.0

Hero WOD's

Introduction

WOD's are quickly becoming a big part of the training program of choice for the Military, law enforcement, firefighters and others. Since its early days, this special fitness program has embraced the men and women in uniform and it honors the heroes who have died protecting our lives and our countries.

The hero WOD's are the most intense workouts that you'll experience. They are designed to be very intense in honor of the fallen heroes.

Good luck!

The List of WODs

- ➢ Adambrown (39)
- ➢ Adrian (39)
- ➢ Arbate (39)
- ➢ Arnie (40)
- ➢ Badger (40)
- ➢ Barraza (41)
- ➢ Blake (41)
- ➢ Bradley (41)
- ➢ Bradshaw (42)
- ➢ Brehm (42)
- ➢ Brenton (42)
- ➢ Brian (43)
- ➢ Bulger (43)
- ➢ Bull (43)
- ➢ Cameron (44)
- ➢ Carse (44)
- ➢ Clovis (45)
- ➢ COE (45)
- ➢ Collin (45)
- ➢ DaeHan (45)
- ➢ Daniel (46)
- ➢ Danny (46)
- ➢ Del (47)
- ➢ Desforges (47)
- ➢ DT (47)
- ➢ Erin (48)
- ➢ Forrest (48)
- ➢ Garett (48)
- ➢ Gator (49)
- ➢ Glen (49)
- ➢ Griff (49)
- ➢ Hamilton (50)

- ➢ Hammer (50)
- ➢ Hansen (50)
- ➢ Helton (51)
- ➢ Hidalgo (51)
- ➢ Holbrook (52)
- ➢ Holleyman (52)
- ➢ Hortman (52)
- ➢ J.J. (53)
- ➢ Jack (54)
- ➢ JAG 28 (54)
- ➢ Jared (54)
- ➢ Jason (55)
- ➢ Jerry (55)
- ➢ Johnson (55)
- ➢ Jorge (56)
- ➢ Josh (56)
- ➢ Joshie (57)
- ➢ Mr. Joshua (57)
- ➢ JT (57)
- ➢ Klepto (58)
- ➢ Ledesma (58)
- ➢ Loredo (58)
- ➢ Luce (59)
- ➢ Lumberjack 20 (59)
- ➢ Manion (60)
- ➢ McCluskey (60)
- ➢ McGhee (60)
- ➢ Meadows (61)
- ➢ Michael (61)
- ➢ Moon (62)
- ➢ Moore (62)
- ➢ Morrison (62)
- ➢ Murph (63)

- ➢ Nate (63)
- ➢ Nick (63)
- ➢ Nutts (64)
- ➢ Paul (64)
- ➢ Pheezy (64)
- ➢ Rahoi (65)
- ➢ Ralph (65)
- ➢ Randy (65)
- ➢ Rankel (66)
- ➢ Ricky (66)
- ➢ RJ (66)
- ➢ Roy (67)
- ➢ Ryan (67)
- ➢ Santiago (67)
- ➢ Santora (68)
- ➢ Sean (68)
- ➢ TheSeven (68)
- ➢ Severin (69)
- ➢ Ship (69)
- ➢ Small (69)
- ➢ Stephen (70)
- ➢ Strange (70)
- ➢ Thompson (70)
- ➢ Tom (71)
- ➢ Tommy V (71)
- ➢ Tully (72)
- ➢ Tumilson (72)
- ➢ Tyler (72)
- ➢ WarFrank (72)
- ➢ Weaver (73)
- ➢ Weston (73)
- ➢ White (74)
- ➢ Whitten (74)

- ➢ Wilmot (74)
- ➢ Wittman (75)
- ➢ Wood (75)
- ➢ Zeus (75)
- ➢ Zimmerman (76)

Adambrown

295 pound Deadlift, 24 reps

24 Box jumps, 24 inch box

24 Wallball shots, 20 pound ball

195 pound Bench press, 24 reps

24 Box jumps, 24 inch box

24 Wallball shots, 20 pound ball

145 pound Clean, 24 reps

Goal: Complete for time.

Instructions: Complete **2 rounds** for time.

Adrian

3 Forward rolls

5 Wall climbs

7 Toes to bar

9 Box jumps, 30" box

Goal: Complete for time.

Instructions: Complete **7 rounds** as quickly as possible.

Arbate

Run 1 mile

155 pound Clean and jerk, 21 reps

Run 800 meters

155 pound Clean and jerk, 21 reps

Run 1 Mile

Goal: Complete for time.

Instructions: Complete all exercises and movements as quickly as possible.

Arnie

With a single 2 pood kettlebell:

21 Turkish get-ups, Right arm

50 Swings

21 Overhead squats, Left arm

50 Swings

21 Overhead squats, Right arm

50 Swings

21 Turkish get-ups, Left arm

Goal: Complete for time

Instructions: Complete the exercises listed above with a single 2 pood kettlebell as quickly as possible.

Badger

95 pound Squat clean, 30 reps

30 Pull-ups

Run 800 meters

Goal: Complete for time.

Instructions: Complete **3 rounds** for time.

Barraza

Run 200 meters

275 pound Deadlift, 9 reps

6 Burpee bar muscle-ups

Goal: AMRAP in 18 minutes.

Instructions: Complete as many rounds as possible within 18 minutes.

Blake

100 foot Walking lunge with 45lb plate held overhead

30 Box jump, 24 inch box

20 Wallball shots, 20 pound ball

10 Handstand push-ups

Goal: Complete for time.

Instructions: Complete **4 rounds** of the exercises as quickly as possible.

Bradley

Sprint 100 meters

10 Pull-ups

Sprint 100 meters

10 Burpees

Rest 30 seconds

Goal: Complete for time.

Instructions: Complete **10 rounds** of the exercises as quickly as possible.

Bradshaw

3 Handstand push-ups

225 pound Deadlift, 6 reps

12 Pull-ups

24 Double-unders

Goal: Complete for time.

Instructions: Complete **10 rounds** of the exercises as quickly as possible.

Brehm

15 foot Rope climb, 10 ascents

225 pound Back squat, 20 reps

30 Handstand push-ups

Row 40 calories

Goal: Complete for time.

Instructions: Complete all exercises as quickly as possible.

Brenton

Bear crawl 100 feet

Standing broad-jump, 100 feet

Goal: Complete for time.

Instructions: Do three Burpees after every five broad-jumps. If you've got a twenty pound vest or body armor, wear it. Complete 5 rounds as quickly as possible.

Brian

15 foot Rope climb, 5 ascents

185 pound Back squat, 25 reps

Goal: Complete for time.

Instructions: Complete **3 rounds** as quickly as possible.

Bulger

Run 150 meters

7 Chest to bar pull-ups

135 pound Front squat, 7 reps

7 Handstand push-ups

Goal: Complete for time.

Instructions: Complete **10 rounds** as quickly as possible.

Bull

200 Double-unders

135 pound Overhead squat, 50 reps

50 Pull-ups

Run 1 mile

Goal: Complete for time.

Instructions: Complete **2 rounds** as quickly as possible.

Cameron

50 Walking lunge steps

25 Chest to bar pull-ups

50 Box jumps, 24 inch box

25 Triple-unders

50 Back extensions

25 Ring dips

50 Knees to elbows

25 Wallball "2-fer-1s", 20 pound ball

50 Sit-ups

15 foot Rope climb, 5 ascents

Goal: Complete for time.

Instructions: Complete all exercises as quickly as possible.

Carse

95 pound Squat clean

Double-under

185 pound Deadlift

24" Box jump

Begin each round with a 50 meter Bear crawl.

Goal: Complete for time.

Instructions: Do 21-18-15-12-9-6-3 reps of the exercises.

Clovis

Run 10 miles

150 Burpee pull-ups

Goal: Complete for time.

Instructions: Complete exercises as quickly as possible. Partition the run and burpee pull-ups as needed.

COE

95 pound Thruster, 10 reps

10 Ring push-ups

Goal: Complete for time.

Instructions: Complete **10 rounds** as quickly as possible.

Collin

Carry 50 pound sandbag 400 meters

115 pound Push press, 12 reps

12 Box jumps, 24 inch box

95 pound Sumo deadlift high-pull, 12 reps

Goal: Complete for time.

Instructions: Complete **6 rounds** as quickly as possible.

Dae Han

Run 800 meters with a 45 pound barbell

15 foot Rope climb, 3 ascents

135 pound Thruster, 12 reps

Goal: Complete for time.

Instructions: Complete **3 rounds** as quickly as possible.

Daniel

50 Pull-ups

400 meter run

95 pound Thruster, 21 reps

800 meter run

95 pound Thruster, 21 reps

400 meter run

50 Pull-ups

Goal: Complete for time.

Instructions: Complete the exercises as quickly as possible.

Danny

24" box jump, 30 reps

115 pound push press, 20 reps

30 pull-ups

Goal: Complete as many rounds within time frame.

Instructions: Complete as many rounds as possible within 20 minutes.

Del

25 Burpees

Run 400 meters with a 20 pound medicine ball

25 Weighted pull-ups with a 20 pound dumbbell

Run 400 meters with a 20 pound medicine ball

25 Handstand push-ups

Run 400 meters with a 20 pound medicine ball

25 Chest-to-bar pull-ups

Run 400 meters with a 20 pound medicine ball

25 Burpees

Goal: Complete for time.

Instructions: Complete the exercises as quickly as possible.

Desforges

225 pound Deadlift, 12 reps

20 Pull-ups

135 pound Clean and jerk, 12 reps

20 Knees to elbows

Goal: Complete for time.

Instructions: Complete **5 rounds** as quickly as possible.

DT

155 pound Deadlift, 12 reps

155 pound Hang power clean, 9 reps

155 pound Push jerk, 6 reps

Goal: Complete for time.

Instructions: Complete **5 rounds** as quickly as possible.

Erin

40 pound Dumbbells split clean, 15 reps

21 Pull-ups

Goal: Complete for time.

Instructions: Complete **5 rounds** as quickly as possible.

Forrest

20 L-pull-ups

30 Toes to bar

40 Burpees

Run 800 meters

Goal: Complete for time.

Instructions: Complete **3 rounds** of the exercises as quickly as possible.

Garett

75 Squats

25 Ring handstand push-ups

25 L-pull-ups

Goal: Complete for time.

Instructions: Complete **3 rounds** of exercises listed above for time.

Gator

185 pound Front squat, 5 reps

26 Ring push-ups

Goal: Complete for time.

Instructions: Complete **8 rounds** of the exercises as quickly as possible.

Glen

135 pound Clean and jerk, 30 reps

Run 1 mile

15 foot Rope climb, 10 ascents

Run 1 mile

100 Burpees

Goal: Complete for time.

Instructions: Complete all exercises as quickly as possible.

Griff

Run 800 meters

Run 400 meters backwards

Run 800 meters

Run 400 meters backwards

Goal: Complete for time.

Instructions: Complete runs as quickly as possible.

Hamilton

Row 1000 meters

50 Push-ups

Run 1000 meters

50 Pull-ups

Goal: Complete each round for time.

Instructions: Complete **3 rounds** of the exercises for time.

Hammer

135 pound Power clean, 5 reps

135 pound Front squat, 10 reps

135 pound Jerk, 5 reps

20 Pull-ups

Goal: Complete each round for time.

Instructions: Complete **5 rounds** of the exercises for time. Rest 90 seconds between each round.

Hansen

30 reps, 2 pood Kettlebell swing

30 Burpees

30 Glute-ham sit-ups

Goal: Complete for time.

Instructions: Complete **5 rounds** as quickly as possible.

Helton

Run 800 meters

30 reps, 50 pound dumbbell squat cleans

30 Burpees

Goal: Complete for time.

Instructions: Complete **3 rounds** as quickly as possible.

Hidalgo

Run 2 miles

Rest 2 minutes

135 pound Squat clean, 20 reps

20 Box jump, 24" box

20 Walking lunge steps with 45lb plate held overhead

20 Box jump, 24" box

135 pound Squat clean, 20 reps

Rest 2 minutes

Run 2 miles

Goal: Complete for time.

Instructions: Complete the exercises as quickly as possible. If you've got a twenty pound vest or body armor, wear it.

Holbrook

115 pound Thruster, 5 reps

10 Pull-ups

100 meter Sprint

Rest 1 minute

Goal: Complete for time.

Instructions: Complete **10 rounds** as quickly as possible.

Holleyman

5 Wall ball shots, 20 pound ball

3 Handstand push-ups

225 pound Power clean, 1 rep

Goal: Complete for time.

Instructions: Complete **30 rounds** of the exercises for time.

Hortman

Run 800 meters

80 Squats

8 Muscle-ups

Goal: AMRAP in 45 min.

Instructions: Complete as many reps as possible within 45 minutes.

J.J.

185 pound Squat clean, 1 rep

10 Parallette handstand push-ups

185 pound Squat clean, 2 reps

9 Parallette handstand push-ups

185 pound Squat clean, 3 reps

8 Parallette handstand push-ups

185 pound Squat clean, 4 reps

7 Parallette handstand push-ups

185 pound Squat clean, 5 reps

6 Parallette handstand push-ups

185 pound Squat clean, 6 reps

5 Parallette handstand push-ups

185 pound Squat clean, 7 reps

4 Parallette handstand push-ups

185 pound Squat clean, 8 reps

3 Parallette handstand push-ups

185 pound Squat clean, 9 reps

2 Parallette handstand push-ups

185 pound Squat clean, 10 reps

1 Parallette handstand push-up

Goal: Complete for time.

Instructions: Complete as quickly as possible.

Jack

115 pound Push press, 10 reps

10 KB Swings, 1.5 pood

10 Box jumps, 24 inch box

Goal: Complete as many rounds as possible within time frame.

Instructions: Complete as many rounds of the exercises as possible within 20 minutes.

JAG 28

Run 800 meters

28 Kettlebell swings, 2 pood

28 Strict Pull-ups

28 Kettlebell clean and jerk, 2 pood each

28 Strict Pull-ups

Run 800 meters

Goal: Complete for time.

Instructions: Complete exercises as quickly as possible.

Jared

Run 800 meters

40 Pull-ups

70 Push-ups

Goal: Complete for time.

Instructions: Complete **4 rounds** as quickly as possible.

Jason

100 Squats

5 Muscle-ups

75 Squats

10 Muscle-ups

50 Squats

15 Muscle-ups

25 Squats

20 Muscle-ups

Goal: Complete for time.

Instructions: Complete exercises as quickly as possible.

Jerry

Run 1 mile

Row 2K

Run 1 mile

Goal: Complete for time.

Instructions: Complete the round as quickly as possible, start and end with a one mile run.

Johnson

245 pound Deadlift, 9 reps

8 Muscle-ups

155 pound Squat clean, 9 reps

Goal: Complete as many rounds within time frame.

Instructions: Complete as many rounds as possible within 20 minutes.

Jorge

30 GHD sit-ups

155 pound Squat clean, 15 reps

24 GHD sit-ups

155 pound Squat clean, 12 reps

18 GHD sit-ups

155 pound Squat clean, 9 reps

12 GHD sit-ups

155 pound Squat clean, 6 reps

6 GHD sit-ups

155 pound Squat clean, 3 reps

Goal: Complete for time.

Instructions: Complete all exercises as quickly as possible.

Josh

95 pound Overhead squat, 21 reps

42 Pull-ups

95 pound Overhead squat, 15 reps

30 Pull-ups

95 pound Overhead squat, 9 reps

18 Pull-ups

Goal: Complete for time.

Instructions: Complete exercises as quickly as possible.

Joshie

40 pound Dumbbell snatch, 21 reps, right arm

21 L Pull-ups

40 pound Dumbbell snatch, 21 reps, left arm

21 L Pull-ups

Goal: Complete for time.

Instructions: Complete 3 rounds for time. Note - The snatches are full squat snatches.

Mr. Joshua

Run 400 meters

30 Glute-ham sit-ups

250 pound Deadlift, 15 reps

Goal: Complete for time.

Instructions: Complete **5 rounds** as quickly as possible.

JT

Handstand push-ups

Ring dips

Push-ups

Goal: Complete for time

Instructions: 21-15-9 reps for time.

Klepto

27 Box jumps, 24" box

20 Burpees

11 Squat cleans, 145 pounds

Goal: Complete for time.

Instructions: Complete **4 rounds** of the exercises for time.

Ledesma

5 Parallette handstand push-ups

10 Toes through rings

20 pound Medicine ball cleans, 15 reps

Goal: Complete as many rounds as possible within time frame.

Instructions: Complete as many rounds as possible for the exercises listed above within 20 minutes time frame.

Loredo

24 Squats

24 Push-ups

24 Walking lunge steps

Run 400 meters

Goal: Complete for time.

Instructions: Complete **6 rounds** of the exercises for time.

Luce

Wearing a 20 pound vest:

Run 1K

10 Muscle-ups

100 Squats

Goal: C omplete for time.

Instructions: Complete **3 rounds** of the exercises listed above with a 20 pound vest.

Lumberjack 20

20 Deadlifts (275lbs)

Run 400m

20 KB swings (2pood)

Run 400m

20 Overhead Squats (115lbs)

Run 400m

20 Burpees

Run 400m

20 Pullups (Chest to Bar)

Run 400m

20 Box jumps (24")

Run 400m

20 DB Squat Cleans (45lbs each)

Run 400m

Goal: Complete for time.

Instructions: Complete exercises for time.

Manion

Run 400 meters

135 pound Back squat, 29 reps

Goal: Complete for time.

Instructions: Complete **7 rounds** of the exercises as quickly as possible.

McCluskey

9 Muscle-ups

15 Burpee pull-ups

21 Pull-ups

Run 800 meters

Goal: Complete for time.

Instructions: Perform **3 rounds** of the exercises as quickly as possible.

McGhee

275 pound Deadlift, 5 reps

13 Push-ups

9 Box jumps, 24 inch box

Goal: Complete as many rounds within 30 minutes.

Instructions: Complete as many rounds as possible of the exercises listed above, within a 30 minutes time frame.

Meadows

20 Muscle-ups

25 Lowers from an inverted hang on the rings, slowly, with straight body and arms

30 Ring handstand push-ups

35 Ring rows

40 Ring push-ups

Goal: Complete for time.

Instructions: Complete the exercises as quickly as possible.

Michael

Run 800 meters

50 Back Extensions

50 Sit-ups

Goal: Complete for time.

Instructions: Complete a total of **3 rounds** for time.

Moon

40 pound dumbbell Hang split snatch, 10 reps Right arm

15 ft Rope Climb, 1 ascent

40 pound dumbbell Hang split snatch, 10 reps Left arm

15 ft Rope Climb, 1 ascent

Goal: Complete for time.

Instructions: Complete **7 rounds** as quickly as possible. Alternate feet in the split snatch sets.

Moore

15 ft Rope Climb, 1 ascent

Run 400 meters

Max rep Handstand push-ups

Goal: As many rounds as possible in time frame.

Instructions: Complete as many rounds as possible within 20 minutes.

Morrison

Wall ball shots, 20 pound ball

Box jump, 24 inch box

Kettlebell swings, 1.5 pood

Goal: Complete for time.

Instructions: Complete 50-40-30-20 and 10 rep rounds as quickly as possible.

Murph

1 mile Run

100 Pull-ups

200 Push-ups

300 Squats

1 mile Run

Goal: Complete for time.

Instructions: Partition the pull-ups, push-ups, and squats as needed. Start and finish with a mile run. If you've got a twenty pound vest or body armor, wear it.

Nate

2 Muscle-ups

4 Handstand Push-ups

8 2-Pood Kettlebell swings

Goal: Complete as many rounds as possible within time frame.

Instructions: Complete as many rounds as possible within 20 minutes.

Nick

45 pound Dumbbell hang squat clean, 10 reps

6 Handstand push-ups on dumbbells

Goal: Complete for time.

Instructions: Complete **12 rounds** for time.

Nutts

10 Handstand push-ups

250 pound Deadlift, 15 reps

25 Box jumps, 30 inch box

50 Pull-ups

100 Wallball shots, 20 pounds, 10'

200 Double-unders

Run 400 meters with a 45lb plate

Goal: Complete for time.

Instructions: Complete exercises listed above for time.

Paul

50 Double unders

35 Knees to elbows

185 pound Overhead walk, 20 yards

Goal: Complete for time.

Instructions: Complete **5 rounds** of exercises listed above as quickly as possible.

Pheezy

165 pound Front squat, 5 reps

18 Pull-ups

225 pound Deadlift, 5 reps

18 Toes-to-bar

165 pound Push jerk, 5 reps

18 Hand-release push-ups

Goal: Complete for time.

Instructions: Complete **3 rounds** for time.

Rahoi

24 inch Box Jump, 12 reps

95 pound Thruster, 6 reps

6 Bar-facing burpees

Goal: AMRAP within time time frame.

Instructions: Complete as many reps as possible within 12 minutes.

Ralph

250 pound Deadlift, 8 reps

16 Burpees

15 foot Rope climb, 3 ascents

Run 600 meters

Goal: Complete for time.

Instructions: Complete **5 rounds** as quickly as possible.

Randy

75 power snatch, 75 reps

Goal: Complete for time.

Instructions: Complete 75 power snatches as quickly as possible.

Rankel

225 pound Deadlift, 6 reps

7 Burpee pull-ups

10 Kettlebell swings, 2 pood

Run 200 meters

Goal: AMRAP (As Many Rounds As Possible), 20 Minutes

Instructions: Complete as many rounds as possible within 20 minutes.

Ricky

10 Pull-ups

75 pound dumbbell Deadlift, 5 reps

135 pound Push-press, 8 reps

Goal: Complete as many rounds as possible in time frame.

Instructions: Complete as many rounds as possible within 20 minutes.

RJ

Run 800 meters

15 ft Rope Climb, 5 ascents

50 Push-ups

Goal: Complete for time.

Instructions: Complete **5 rounds** as quickly as possible.

Roy

225 pound Deadlift, 15 reps

20 Box jumps, 24 inch box

25 Pull-ups

Goal: Complete for time.

Instructions: Complete **5 rounds** as quickly as possible.

Ryan

7 Muscle-ups

21 Burpees

Each burpee terminates with a jump one foot above max standing reach.

Goal: Complete for time.

Instructions: Complete **5 rounds** as quickly as possible.

Santiago

35 pound Dumbbell hang squat clean, 18 reps

18 Pull-ups

135 pound Power clean, 10 reps

10 Handstand push-ups

Goal: Complete for time.

Instructions: Complete **7 rounds** as quickly as possible.

Santora

155 pound Squat cleans, 1 minute

20' Shuttle sprints (20' forward + 20' backwards = 1 rep), 1 minute

245 pound Deadlifts, 1 minute

Burpees, 1 minute

155 pound Jerks, 1 minute

Rest 1 minute

Goal: Complete for reps.

Instructions: Complete **3 rounds** for as many reps as possible.

Sean

11 Chest to bar pull-ups

75 pound Front squat, 22 reps

Goal: Complete for time.

Instructions: Complete **10 rounds** of exercises listed above as quickly as possible.

The Seven

7 Handstand push-ups

135 pound Thruster, 7 reps

7 Knees to elbows

245 pound Deadlift, 7 reps

7 Burpees

7 Kettlebell swings, 2 pood

7 Pull-ups

Goal: Complete for time.

Instructions: Complete **7 rounds** of exercises listed above as quickly as possible.

Severin

50 Strict Pull-ups

100 Push-ups, release hands from floor at the bottom

Run 5K

Goal: Complete for time.

Instructions: Complete exercises as quickly as possible. If you've got a twenty pound vest or body armor, wear it.

Ship

185 pound Squat clean, 7 reps

8 Burpee box jumps, 36" box

Goal: Complete for time.

Instructions: Complete **9 rounds** of the exercises as quickly as possible.

Small

Row 1000 meters

50 Burpees

50 Box jumps, 24" box

Run 800 meters

Goal: Complete for time.

Instructions: Complete **3 rounds** of the exercises as quickly as possible.

Stephen

GHD sit-up

Back extension

Knees to elbow

95 pound Stiff legged deadlift

Goal: Complete for time.

Instructions: Perform 30-25-20-15-10-5 rep rounds of the exercises listed above.

Strange

600 meter Run

1.5 pood Weighted pull-up, 11 reps

11 Walking lunge steps, carrying 1.5 pood kettlebells

1.5 pood Kettlebell thruster, 11 reps

Goal: Complete for time.

Instructions: Complete **8 rounds** of the exercises as quickly as possible.

Thompson

15 ft Rope Climb, 1 ascent

95 pound Back squat, 29 reps

135 pound barbells Farmer carry, 10 meters

Goal: Complete for time.

Instructions: Complete **10 rounds** as quickly as possible.Begin the rope climbs seated on the floor.

Tom

7 Muscle-ups

155 pound Thruster, 11 reps

14 Toes-to-bar

Goal: AMRAP in 25 min.

Instructions: Complete as many rounds as possible within 25 minutes.

Tommy V

115 pound Thruster, 21 reps

15 ft Rope Climb, 12 ascents

115 pound Thruster, 15 reps

15 ft Rope Climb, 9 ascents

115 pound Thruster, 9 reps

15 ft Rope Climb, 6 ascents

Goal: Complete for time.

Instructions: Complete all exercises and movements as quickly as possible.

Tully

Swim 200 meters

40 pound Dumbbell squat cleans, 23 reps

Goal: Complete for time.

Instructions: Complete **4 rounds** as quickly as possible.

Tumilson

Run 200 meters

11 Dumbbell burpee deadlifts, 60 pound dumbbells

Goal: Complete for time.

Instructions: Complete **8 rounds** as quickly as possible.

Tyler

7 Muscle-ups

21 reps 95 pound Sumo-deadlift high-pull

Goal: Complete for time.

Instructions: Complete **5 rounds** as quickly as possible.

War Frank

25 Muscle-ups

100 Squats

35 GHD situps

Goal: Complete for time.

Instructions: Complete **3 rounds** of exercises listed above for time.

Weaver

10 L-pull-ups

15 Push-ups

15 Chest to bar Pull-ups

15 Push-ups

20 Pull-ups

15 Push-ups

Goal: Complete for time.

Instructions: Complete **4 rounds** of exercises listed above for time.

Weston

Row 1000 meters

200 meter Farmer carry, 45 pound dumbbells

45 pound dumbbell Waiter walk, 50 meters, Right arm

45 pound dumbbell Waiter walk, 50 meters, Left arm

Goal: Complete for time.

Instructions: Complete **5 rounds** as quickly as possible.

White

15' Rope climb, 3 ascents

10 Toes to bar

21 Walking lunge steps with 45lb plate held overhead

Run 400 meters

Goal: Complete for time.

Instructions: Complete **5 rounds** as quickly as possible.

Whitten

22 Kettlebell swings, 2 pood

22 Box jump, 24 inch box

Run 400 meters

22 Burpees

22 Wall ball shots, 20 pound ball

Goal: Complete for time.

Instructions: Complete **5 rounds** as quickly as possible.

Wilmot

50 Squats

25 Ring dips

Goal: Complete for time.

Instructions: Complete **6 rounds** of the exercises as quickly as possible.

Wittman

1.5 pood Kettlebell swing, 15 reps

95 pound Power clean, 15 reps

15 Box jumps, 24" box

Goal: Complete for time.

Instructions: Complete **7 rounds** of the exercises as quickly as possible.

Wood

Run 400 meters

10 Burpee box jumps, 24" box

95 pound Sumo-deadlift high-pull, 10 reps

95 pound Thruster, 10 reps

Rest 1 minute

Goal: Complete for time.

Instructions: Complete **5 rounds** of the exercises as quickly as possible.

Zeus

30 Wall ball shots, 20 pound ball

75 pound Sumo deadlift high-pull, 30 reps

30 Box jump, 20" box

75 pound Push press, 30 reps

Row 30 calories

30 Push-ups

Body weight Back squat, 10 reps

Goal: Complete for time.

Instructions: Complete **3 rounds** of the exercises as quickly as possible.

Zimmerman

11 Chest-to-bar pull-ups

2 Deadlifts, 315 pounds

10 Handstand push-ups

Goal: AMRAP in time frame.

Instructions: Complete as many rounds as possible within 25 minutes.

WOD's 2.0

WODs-To-Go: WOD's that don't require equipment

Introduction

These are WOD's that can be done on your own with little or no use of equipment. With these workouts, there's little excuse that can be made whilst you're travelling, or on vacation, or at home without equipment. WOD's don't need any equipment to be effective which is one of the best things about it. All you need for these WOD's is effort, some time and space, a device to keep time and you are good to go!

As many of these WOD's have no "official names", they have been named after the main exercises that they include and also they have been numbered. That way it will be easier for you to repeatedly access them when you need to.

The List of WODs

1. 10 squats, 10 push-ups (82)

2. 10 sit-ups, 10 burpees (82)

3. 10 push-ups, 10 air squats, 10 sit-ups (82)

4. 10 hand stand push-ups, 200m run (82)

5. 10 burpees, 100m sprint (83)

6. 10 push-ups, 100m sprint (83)

7. 100 air squats (83)

8. 100 burpees (83)

9. 250 jumping jacks (84)

10. 100 jumping jacks, 50 push-ups, 75 air squats, 25 burpees (84)

11. 10 vertical jumps, 400m run (84)

12. 100m sprint, 100m walk (85)

13. 10 high vertical jumps, 10 push-ups (85)

14. 50 air squats (85)

15. 5 pushups, 5 sit ups, 5 squats (85)

16. Mountain Climbers, Supermans, Lunges, Cross-Overs (86)

17. Burpees, Squats, Knees-to-chin (86)

18. Broad Jump Burpees, Jumping Lunges, Leg Lifts (86)

19. Run, Push-ups, Sit-ups, Squats, Run (87)

20. Bench jumps, jumping pull-ups, jump squats, In-and-outs (87)

21. Knees-to-Elbow, Bench Jump Burpees, Cross-Overs, Squats (87)

22. Bear crawl, Push-ups, Jumps, Lunges and more..(88)

23. Max push-ups, sit-ups, squats (88)

24. Lunges, squats, psuh-ups (89)

25. Burpies and sit-ups (89)

26. Tabata WOD (89)

27. Burpees, Push-ups, Squats (90)

28. Box jumps, burpees (90)

29. 100m sprint, 10 burpees (90)

30. Push-ups, hand stands (90)

31. Vertical jumps, squats, long jumps (91)

32. Squats, push-ups burpees (91)

33. Airs quats, Burpies, Push-Ups (91)

34. The "Susan" (92)

35. Burpees and sit ups (ladder) (92)

36. Sit ups, push-ups and 100m sprint (ladder) (92)

37. One mile run (93)

38. 100 burpies (93)

39. 100 push-ups (93)

40. Handstand, air squats (93)

41. 1 mile run, squats (93)

42. 100m sprint, squats (94)

43. 100m sprint, air squats (94)

44. Run 400m, air squats (94)

45. Handstand (95)

46. Walk on your hands (95)

47. Vertical jumps, push-ups (95)

48. 200m sprint, 25 push-ups (95)

49. Invisible Fran (96)

50. 1 mile run, squats (96)

1. 10 squats,10 push-ups

10 push ups

10 squats

Goal: Complete for time.

Instructions: Complete **10 rounds** of each exercise as quickly as possible.

2. 10 sit-ups, 10 burpees

10 sit-ups

10 burpees

Goal: Complete for time.

Instructions: Complete **10 rounds** of each exercise as quickly as possible.

3. 10 push-ups, 10 air squats, 10 sit-ups

10 push-ups

10 air squats

10 sit-ups

Goal: Complete for time

Instructions: Complete **6 rounds** as quickly as possible.

4. 10 handstand push-ups, 200m run

10 handstand push-ups

200 meter run

Goal: Complete for time

Instructions: Complete a total of **3 rounds** of each as quickly as possible.

5. 10 burpees, 100m sprint

10 burpees

100meter sprint

Goal: Complete for time.

Instructions: Complete **10 rounds** as quickly as possible.

6. 10 push-ups, 100m sprint

10 push-ups

100meter sprint

Goal: Complete for time.

Instructions: Complete **10 rounds** as quickly as possible.

7. 100 air squats

100 air squats

Goal: Complete for time.

Instructions: Complete 100 air squats as quickly as possible.

8. 100 burpees

100 burpees

Goal: Complete for time.

Instructions: Complete 100 burpees as quickly as possible.

9. 250 jumping jacks

250 jumping jacks

Goal: Complete for time.

Instructions: Complete 250 jumping jacks as quickly as possible.

10. 100 jumping jacks, 50 push-ups, 75 air squats, 25 burpees

100 jumping jacks

50 push-ups

75 air squats

25 burpees

Goal: Complete for time.

Instructions: Complete all reps of all exercises as quickly as possible.

11. 10 vertical jumps, 400m run

10 vertical jumps

400 meter run

Goal: Complete for time.

Instructions: Complete **5 rounds** as quickly as possible.

12. 100m sprint, 100m walk

100m sprint

100m walk

Goal: Complete for time.

Instructions: Complete **10 rounds** of exercises as quickly as possible.

13. 10 high vertical jumps, 10 push-ups

10 vertical jumps as high as you can

10 push-ups

Goal: Complete for time.

Instructions: Complete **5 rounds** as quickly as possible.

14. 50 air squats

50 air squats

Goal: Complete for time.

Instructions: Complete **4 rounds** of 50 air squats, rest a couple of minutes between each round.

15. 5 push ups, 5 sit ups, 5 squats

5 push-ups

5 sit-ups

5 squats

Goal: Complete for time.

Instructions: Complete **20 rounds** for time.

16. Mountain Climbers, Supermans, Lunges, Cross-Overs

20 Mountain Climbers

20 Supermans

20 Lunges

20 Cross-Overs

Goal: Complete for time.

Instructions: Complete **5 rounds** for time.

17. Burpees, Squats, Knees-to-chin

10 Burpees

15 Squats

20 Knees-to-chin

Goal: Complete as many rounds as possible within time frame.

Instructions: Complete as many rounds of the exercisesas possible within 30 minutes.

18.Broad Jump Burpees, Jumping Lunges, Leg Lifts

10 Broad Jump Burpees

10 Jumping Lunges

10 Leg Lifts

Goal: Complete for time.

Instructions: Complete **10 rounds** as quickly as possible.

19. Run, Push-ups, Sit-ups, Squats, Run

10 minute Run

100 Push-ups

200 Sit-ups

300 Squats

5 minute Run

Goal: Complete for time.

Instructions: Complete all reps of all exercises as quickly as possible, starting and ending with a run.

20. Bench jumps, jumping pull-ups, jump squats, In-and-outs

25 Bench Jumps (or Step-ups if a bench is not avaliable)

25 Jumping Pull-ups

25 Jump Squats

25 In-and-outs

Goal: Complete for time.

Instructions: Complete **4 rounds** as quickly as possible.

21. Knees-to-Elbow, Bench Jump Burpees, Cross-Overs, Squats

10 Knees-to-Elbow (substitute 20 knees-to-chin if unable to to K2E)

15 Bench Jump Burpees

20 Cross-Overs

25 Squats

Goal: Complete for time.

Instructions: Complete **4 rounds** as quickly as possible.

22. Bear crawl, Push-ups, Jumps, Lunges and more..

15m Bear Crawl

20 Push-ups

15m Crab Walk

20 Cross-overs

15m Lunge Walk

20 Jump Squats

15m Broad Jump Burpees

20 Mountain Climbers

Goal: Complete for time.

Instructions: Complete **5 rounds** as quickly as possible.

23. Max push-ups, sit-ups, squats

2 minute max push ups

1 minute break

2 minues max sit ups

1 minute break

2 minute max squats

Goal: Complete as many reps as possible.

Instructions: Complete as many reps of the exercises as possible. rest 1 minute between each exercise.

24. Lunges, squats, psuh-ups

Lunge 20 steps

20 squats

10 pushups

Goal: Complete for time.

Instructions: Complete **5 rounds** for time.

25. Burpies and sit-ups

10 burpies

10 sit-ups

Goals: Complete for time.

Instructions: Complete **10 rounds** as quickly as possible.

26. Tabata WOD

Tabata squat

Tabata pushup

Tabata situp

Tabata over head press (you can press anything, just your hands too)

Goal: Complete for reps.

Instructions: Complete a total of 8 times of 20 seconds of work 10 seconds of rest of the exercises.

27. Burpees, Push-ups, Squats

3 Burpees

4 pushups

5 squats

Goal: As many reps as possible.

Instructions: Complete as many reps as possible within 10 minutes.

28. Box jumps, burpees

50 box jumps (or step jumps if box unavaliable)

10 burpees

Goal: Complete for time.

Instructions: Complete **5 rounds** as quickly as possible.

29. 100m sprint, 10 burpees

100 meter sprint

10 burpees

Goal: Complete for time.

Instructions: Complete **10 rounds** as quickly as possible.

30. Push-ups, handstands

30 push-ups

30 second handstand

Goal: Complete for time.

Instructions: Complete **10 rounds** as quickly as possible.

31. Vertical jumps, squats, long jumps

3 vertical jumps

3 squats

3 long jumps

Goal: Complete for time.

Instructions: Complete **5 rounds** for time. Rest as much as necessary.

32. Squats, push-ups burpees

7 squats

7 push-ups

7 burpees

Goal: Complete for time

Instructions: Complete **7 rounds** as quickly as possible.

33. Air squats, Burpies, Push-Ups

20 Air squats

20 Burpees

20 Push-ups

Goal: Complete for time.

Instructions: Complete **3 rounds** of the exercises as quickly as possible.

34. The "Susan"

Run 200m

10 squats

10 push ups

Goal: Complete for time.

Instructions: Complete **5 rounds** of the exercises as quickly as possible.

35. Burpees and sit ups (ladder).

Burpees

Sit ups

Goal: Complete for time.

Instructions: Complete 10 to 1 ladder reps (1st set – 10 reps, 2nd set- 9 reps etc.) of the exercises.

36. Sit ups, push ups and 100m sprint (ladder).

Sit ups

Push ups

100 meter sprint

Goal: Complete for time.

Instructions: Complete 10 to 1 ladder reps (1st set – 10 reps, 2nd set- 9 reps etc.) of the exercises.

37. One mile run

1 mile run

Goal: Complete for time.

Instructions: Run 1 mile as quickly as possible.

38. 100 burpies

100 burpies

Goal: Complete for time.

Instructions: Complete 100 burpies as quickly as possible.

39. 100 push ups

100 push ups

Goal: Complete for time.

Instructions: Complete 100 push ups as quickly as possible.

40. Handstand, air squats.

30 second handstand

20 air squats

Goal: Complete for time.

Instructions: Complete **5 rounds** as quickly as possible.

41. 1 mile run, squats

1 mile run

50 Squats

Goal: Complete for time.

Instructions: Run 1 mile for time and then do 50 squats for time (1 round).

42. 100m sprint, squats

100 meter sprint

30 Squats

Goal: Complete for time.

Instructions: Complete **6 rounds** of the exercises as quickly as possible.

43. 100m sprint, air squats

100 meter sprint

30 Air squats

Goal: Complete for time.

Instructions: Complete **8 rounds** of the exercises as quickly as possible.

44. Run 400m, air squats

400 meter run

50 Air squats

Goal: Complete for time.

Instructions: Complete **4 rounds** as quickly as possible.

45. Handstand

3 minute headstand

Goal: Keep a good form (as much as possible).

Instructions: Do a 3 minute handstand with as good of a form as possible.

46. Walk on your hands

Walk 100meters on your hands

Goal: Complete exercise with stopping as little as possible.

Instructions: Walk 100 meters on yours hands with stopping as few times as possible. Do it even if you can do it 2 meters at a time.

47. Vertical jumps, push-ups

10 vertical jumps

10 push-ups

Goal: Complete for time.

Instructions: Complete 5 rounds as quickly as possible.

48. 200m sprint, 25 push-ups

200 meter sprint

25 push-ups

Goal: Complete for time.

Instructions: Do **3 rounds** as quickly as possible.

49. Invisible Fran

21-15-9 reps of

Air squats

Push-ups

Goal: Complete for time.

Instructions: Do 21-15-9 reps of the exercises as quickly as possible.

50. 1 mile run, squats

1 mile run

10 squats every minute while running the 1 mile run

Goal: Complete for time.

Instructions: While running 1 mile, stop every minute and do 10 squats. Complete as quickly as possible.

WOD's 2.0

Final Thoughts

Now you are all set to get fit with WOD's! WOD's are part of a unique physical fitness program which you really do need to experience. This book contains a very large variety of great WOD's for every level of experience. Now it's time to immerse yourself in the world of fitness and experience the amazing WOD's. Feel free to modify the reps (increase or decrease the repetitions) to better fit your level of fitness. Get started at home, your local park or your local "cross-training box" and feel the difference between WOD's and different types of workouts and fitness programs.

You are more than welcome to join the *WODs 2.0* facebook page here: *facebook.com/WODs2*

Motivational Quotes

Here are some great motivational quotes and videos to inspire you and help you to complete the WOD's! Whenever you're feeling down, like missing a workout or you just in need of a mental boost, come here to get motivated!

"Pain is only temporary but victory is forever."

- Jeremy H.

"Winning means you're willing to go longer, work harder, and give more than anyone else. "

- Vince Lombardi

"Winners don't wait for chances, they take them."

- Unknown

"Love is playing every game as if it's your last. "

- Michael Jordan

"There is no glory in practice, but without practice, there is no glory... "

- Unknown

"Champions aren't made in the gyms. Champions are made from something they have deep inside them -- a desire, a dream, a vision. "

- Muhammad Ali

"The vision of a champion is someone who is bent over, drenched in sweat, at the point of exhaustion when no one else is watching"

- Anson Dorrance

"You and your opponent want the same thing. The only thing that matters is who works the hardest for it. "

-Unknown

"You don't always get what you wish for, you get what you work for "

- Unknown

"The best athletes in the world are those who are willing to push harder then anyone else, and go through more pain then anyone else. "

- Ashley M.L.

"Winning is not a sometime thing; it's an all time thing. You don't win once in a while, you don't do things right once in a while......you do them right all the time. Winning is a habit. Unfortunately, so is losing. "

- Vince Lombardi

"It's supposed to be hard. If it wasn't hard, everyone would do it. The hard is what makes it great. "

- Tom Hanks, A League of Their Own

"If you only ever give 90% in training then you will only ever give 90% when it matters"

- Michael Owen

"Every time you stay out late; every time you sleep in; every time you miss a workout; every time you don't give 100%... you make it that much easier for me to beat you."

- Unknown

"Good, better, best. Never let it rest. Until your good is better and your better is best."

- Tim Duncan

"Victory belongs to the most persevering."

- Napoleon

"It's not whether you get knocked down; it's whether you get up."

– Vince Lombardi

"I've missed more than 9,000 shots in my career. I've lost almost 300 games. 26 times, I've been trusted to take the game winning shot and missed. I've failed over and over and over again in my life. And that is why I succeed."

– Michael Jordan

"Gold medals aren't really made of gold. They're made of sweat, determination, and a hard-to-find alloy called guts."

– Dan Gable

"The highest compliment that you can pay me is to say that I work hard every day, that I never dog it."

– Wayne Gretzky

"You miss 100 percent of the shots you don't take."

– Wayne Gretzky

"Never give up! Failure and rejection are only the first step to succeeding."

– Jim Valvano

"You're never a loser until you quit trying."

– Mike Ditka

"A champion is someone who gets up when he can't."

– Jack Dempsey

"I hated every minute of training, but I said, 'Don't quit. Suffer now and live the rest of your life as a champion.'"

– Muhammad Ali

"It is not the size of a man but the size of his heart that matters."

– Evander Holyfield

"Never let your head hang down. Never give up and sit down and grieve. Find another way."

– Satchel Paige

"Pain is temporary. It may last a minute, or an hour, or a day, or a year, but eventually it will subside and something else will take its place. If I quit, however, it lasts forever."

– Lance Armstrong

"You can't put a limit on anything. The more you dream, the farther you get."

– Michael Phelps

"Push yourself again and again. Don't give an inch until the final buzzer sounds."

– Larry Bird

"What do do with a mistake: recognize it, admit it, learn from it, forget it."

– Dean Smith

"If you have everything under control, you're not moving fast enough."

– Mario Andretti

"Win If You Can, Lose If You Must, But NEVER QUIT!"

– Cameron Trammell

"Without self-discipline, success is impossible, period."

– Lou Holtz

"If you can believe it, the mind can achieve it."

– Ronnie Lott

"The mind is the limit. As long as the mind can envision the fact that you can do something, you can do it, as long as you really believe 100 percent."

– Arnold Schwarzenegger

6204428R00059

Printed in Great Britain
by Amazon.co.uk, Ltd.,
Marston Gate.